W9-DCB-545

THE HUMAN BODY

The Circulatory System

Susan Glass

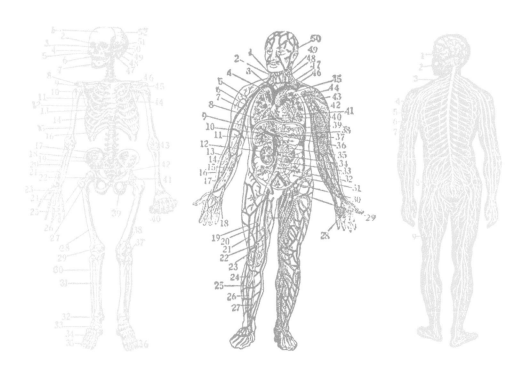

PERFECTION LEARNING®

Editorial Director:	Susan C. Thies
Editor:	Mary L. Bush
Design Director:	Randy Messer
Book Design:	Brianne Osborn
	Emily J. Greazel
Cover Design:	Michael A. Aspengren

A special thanks to the following for their scientific review of the book:

Paul Pistek, Instructor of Biological Sciences, North Iowa Area Community College

Jeffrey Bush, Field Engineer, Vessco, Inc.

Image Credits:

© Argosy Illustration: pp. 24, 30, 39; © Charles O'Rear/CORBIS: p. 16; © Jim Zuckerman/CORBIS: cover (background), p. 27; © Science Pictures Limited/CORBIS: p. 28; © Lester V. Bergman/CORBIS: p. 29; © Tom & Dee Ann McCarthy/CORBIS: p. 38

ClipArt.com: pp. 1, 3, 4, 6 (background), 11 (bottom), 15, 18, 20, 26, 32, 36, 40, 42, 46, 47, 48; Image Library: pp. 11 (top), 37; LifeART © 2003 Lippincott, Williams, & Wilkins: cover (bottom center, bottom right) pp. 5, 6 (foreground), 8 (right), 12, 13, 14, 19, 22, 23; Perfection Learning Corporation: p. 21; Photos.com: cover (bottom left), back cover, pp. 7, 8 (left), 9, 10, 17, 25, 33, 35, 41, 43, 45

Perfection Learning® Corporation
1000 North Second Avenue, P.O. Box 500
Logan, Iowa 51546-0500.
Phone: 1-800-831-4190
Fax: 1-800-543-2745
perfectionlearning.com

5 6 7 8 9 10 PP 13 12 11 10 09 08

PB ISBN-10: 0-7891-6077-3 ISBN-13: 978-0-7891-6077-5
RLB ISBN-10: 0-7569-4458-9 ISBN-13: 978-0-7569-4458-2

Contents

Introduction
Let's Circulate

Have you ever heard the expression "what goes around comes around"? *Circulate* means "to move around in a circle back to a starting point." In your circulatory system, what goes around—your **blood**—does indeed come around. In fact, your blood goes and comes around your body about 1000 times a day. That's why it's called the *circulatory system*.

Adults have about 1.3 gallons of blood in their bodies. If it circulates 1000 times a day, that's about 1300 gallons of blood moving through the body each day!

Try This!

See how much blood an adult has in his or her body. Find an empty gallon milk jug. Fill it with water and pour it into a large bowl or empty sink. Then measure 5 cups of water, and pour it into the bowl or sink. This is about how much blood is in an adult's body.

The Circulatory System

What circulates the blood through your body? Your **heart** is the mighty muscle pump that pushes the blood around your body. Pounding away in the center of your chest, the heart is an unstoppable beating machine. If you live an average lifetime, your heart will have beaten over two billion times!

How Long Will You Live?

No one really knows how long you'll live, but the average life span in America is about 77. So you have a long life ahead of you!

Blood vessels carry the blood that your heart pumps. These tiny tubes work with your heart to deliver blood to the body.

The circulatory system is made up of the heart, the blood vessels, and the blood. These three parts work day and night, never taking a vacation or even a TV break.

The circulatory system works closely with the respiratory, or breathing, system. Blood picks up oxygen from the lungs and drops it off throughout the body. When the blood runs out of fresh oxygen, it returns to the heart so it can be pumped to the lungs for a fill-up. The heart and lungs work side by side to keep your body supplied with the oxygen it needs.

The circulatory system is so quick that it takes blood only a little more than a minute to circulate once through the heart, lungs, and body. That's a lot of circulating in a lifetime!

The whole circulatory system is impressive, but let's start with the center, or as some might say, the "heart" of it.

Your Beating Heart

The word *heart* is used in a lot of expressions. If you have "a lot of heart," you have spirit, dedication, or courage. If you've memorized something, you "know it by heart." Jealous people are said to "eat their hearts out" when others have something they want. Kids "cross their hearts" to show that they are telling the truth (supposedly). If something makes you happy, it "does your heart good" or "warms your heart." Kind people "have their hearts in the right place." You might even try to talk your teacher into giving you a passing grade by telling her to "have a heart."

Often the word *heart* is used to talk about love and relationships. If you've "lost your heart," you've fallen in love. You might say your "heart skips a beat" when you see that special person. You might "win the heart" of a cute guy or girl by taking them to a scary, "heart-stopping" movie and having a "heart-to-heart" talk afterward. If everyone can tell how you feel about someone, you're "wearing your heart on your sleeve." And when someone doesn't return your feelings, he or she has "broken your heart."

We say that people have big hearts, kind hearts, hard hearts, soft hearts, heavy hearts, light hearts, hearts of stone, and hearts of gold.

If the heart is just a pump for moving blood around, then why do we use it in so many expressions? Maybe it's because the heart is so important to our bodies. Or perhaps it's because people have always noticed that the heart speeds up when someone is excited, or angry, or afraid. At one time, people even believed that the heart was the home of all thoughts and feelings. Whatever the reason, the heart has a permanent place in our language as well as our bodies.

Heart History

Hundreds of years ago, people didn't know how the body worked. Ancient Egyptians thought the heart was the center of emotion and intelligence. The ancient Greeks believed a person's spirit was found in the heart. These ideas were handed down over the centuries, and the heart became linked with feelings and thoughts. In time, however, scientists came to understand that it is actually the brain that is the center of emotions, intelligence, hopes, dreams, and love. In spite of this, the heart expressions have remained. After all, it would seem silly to say that someone without feelings is "brainless" or someone has a "brain of gold."

A Valentine Heart?

When you draw a heart, what do you draw? Most people draw the symbol that has come to mean "heart." It's on every valentine card or love note. But your real heart doesn't look like a valentine heart. It looks more like a big chunk of meat with tubes sticking out of the top. It's about the same shape and size as your fist.

Your heart weighs about as much as a tennis shoe. The average weight of the heart in a female is 9 ounces. An average male's heart weighs 10.5 ounces.

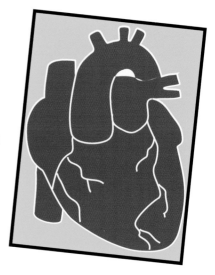

Beat This!

The heart works harder than any other muscle in your body. It started beating well before you were born and hasn't taken a break since.

Try This!

Use a tennis ball to get an idea of how hard your heart works. Squeeze the ball tightly with one hand. It takes about as much effort to do this as it takes your heart to pump blood through your body. Squeeze the ball about once each second for a minute. (This is actually a bit slower than your real heartbeat.) How does your hand feel after a minute? Hard work, isn't it?

How does the heart beat? First your heart expands, or fills up, with blood coming in through the vessels. Then it contracts, or squeezes tight, to push the blood into the lungs. At the same time, blood coming into the heart from the lungs is squeezed out to begin its trip through the body. With each beat, the heart squeezes out enough blood to fill slightly less than half a soda can.

Try This!

Put your hands into a bowl or sink filled with water. Cup your hands together, and let them fill up with water. Lift your hands out of the water, and squeeze them together. Watch the water squirt out. This squeezing and squirting action is similar to how your heart pumps blood.

How fast does your heart beat? It depends on your age. A child's heart beats faster than an adult's because growing takes a lot of energy. The heart and blood deliver this energy. As you grow, your heartbeat changes to meet your energy needs. A newborn baby's heart beats around 130 to 150 times a minute. Six-year-olds average around 100 beats a minute. A ten-year-old's heart beats about 90 beats a minute. An adult's average heartbeat is 72 beats a minute.

Since your body needs more oxygen when it works harder, your heart beats faster. The more energy you use up, the more energy your blood needs to supply. So your heart pumps faster to keep fresh, oxygen-rich blood moving through your body quickly. Your heart beats slowest when you're lying down resting or sleeping.

Try This!

You can listen to a partner's heart using a paper cup. Tear or cut out the bottom of the cup. Put the top of the cup over the person's heart. Press your ear to the other end of the cup, and listen to the beat. You can do this without a cup by just resting your ear on the person's chest over the heart.

Listen to your partner's heart while he or she is lying down and then sitting up. Ask your partner to jog in place for a minute and listen again. How does the heartbeat change?

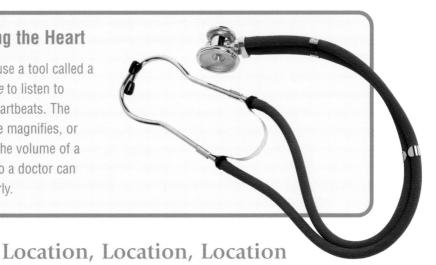

Location, Location, Location

When someone asks you to place your hand over your heart, where do you put your hand? Your heart is located in the middle of your chest, tilted to the left side. If you drew a line down the center of your body, two-thirds of your heart would be on the left side of the line. One-third would be on the right side. The heart sits between the lungs, which is convenient for speedy oxygen pickup.

The heart is well protected by your ribs and breastbone. It is also packaged in a loose sack called the *pericardium*. The pericardium keeps the heart from rubbing against the chest wall as it beats.

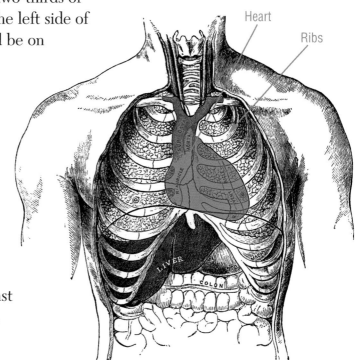

Heart

Ribs

Two Sides to the Story

The heart is a hollow muscle that fills up with blood and then squeezes it out with every beat. Many people think of the heart as a single pump, but your heart is really two pumps working side by side. The right side pumps blood to the lungs to pick up oxygen and drop off carbon dioxide. The left side pumps the oxygen-filled blood that just came back from the lungs to the rest of the body. So there are two loops in your circulation. One loop runs from the heart to the lungs and back. The other loop runs from the heart to the rest of the body and back.

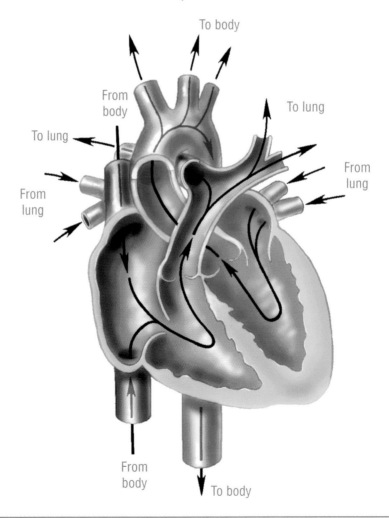

The two sides of the heart are divided by a thick wall called the *septum*. Each side of the heart has two chambers, or hollow spaces. The upper chambers are the right **atrium** and the left atrium. Each atrium is a small, thin-walled area. When blood flows into the heart from either the body or the lungs, it flows into an atrium. There it collects for a moment before being squeezed into a big pumping chamber below.

These large pumping chambers are the **ventricles**. You have a right and a left ventricle. The ventricles contract, or tighten, and push blood out of the heart to the lungs or body.

Rooms in the Heart

The word *atrium* means "entry room." Each atrium is like an entry room to the heart. The right atrium welcomes blood from the body. The left atrium greets blood from the lungs. The plural form of *atrium* is *atria*.

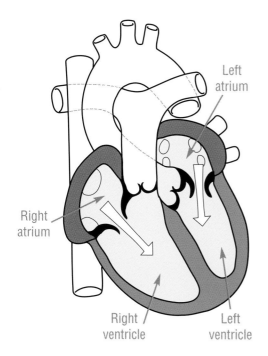

The thin walls of the right and left atria squeeze blood into the ventricles. The valves between each atrium and the ventricle below prevent a backflow of blood.

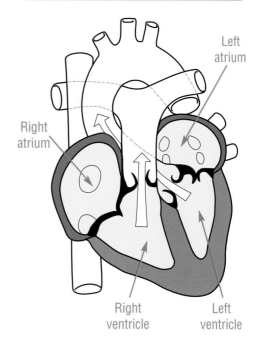

A much stronger heart contraction pushes blood up out of the ventricles and into the arteries.

On the Right Side

The blood that enters the right side of the heart is a dark purplish red. That's because it has dropped off its oxygen load at the **cells** around the body. Oxygen-poor blood is this dark red color. This blood is carrying carbon dioxide and other wastes that it has picked up from the cells.

After collecting for a moment in the right atrium, the blood gets squeezed through a valve down to the right ventricle. A valve is a flap of tissue that acts like a door that only opens one way.

The right ventricle contracts and squeezes the blood out through a big blood vessel leading to the lungs. This blood vessel is the pulmonary **artery**. The pulmonary artery carries the blood into the lungs. Here, the blood drops off the waste materials and picks up a fresh supply of oxygen.

Lub-Dub, Lub-Dub

What are you hearing when you listen to someone's heartbeat? The "lub-dub, lub-dub" sound is actually the sound of the valves closing.

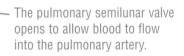

The pulmonary semilunar valve opens to allow blood to flow into the pulmonary artery.

The aortic semilunar valve opens to allow blood to flow into the aorta.

The tricuspid valve opens to let blood flow into the right ventricle. The three flaps of this valve allow blood to flow into the ventricle but prevent the blood from flowing back into the atrium.

The bicuspid valve, also known as the mitral valve, allows blood to flow from the left atrium into the left ventricle.

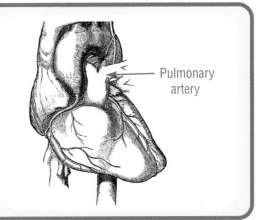

Pulmonary artery

On the Left Side

With a fresh supply of oxygen, the blood returning to the heart from the lungs is now a bright red color. This red blood circles back to the left side of the heart through the pulmonary **vein**. It collects in the left atrium for a moment. Then it gets pushed through a valve down to the left ventricle.

The left ventricle is the most powerful chamber in the heart. It has bigger and stronger muscle walls than the right ventricle. It needs these muscles for its huge job.

The right side of the heart only has to pump hard enough for the blood to travel the short distance to the lungs. The left side of the heart has to push hard enough for the blood to reach the rest of the body. The left ventricle pushes about six times harder than the right ventricle.

The left ventricle pumps blood upward out of the heart. From there the blood travels throughout the body, delivering oxygen and picking up waste. Then it heads back to the right side of the heart to begin its circulatory journey again.

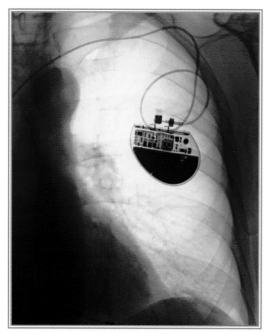

The first artificial pacemakers were powered by a battery that needed to be replaced every four or five years. Since the 1970s, surgeons have implanted pacemakers with rechargeable batteries that last a lifetime.

A Mighty Muscle

The heart is made of a special kind of muscle called *cardiac muscle*. Cardiac muscle beats automatically. A special part of the heart in the right atrium acts as a **pacemaker**. It fires off an electrical impulse, or signal, that makes the muscles in both atria tighten. The impulse is sent to the ventricles, and they also contract. If something goes wrong and the pacemaker that you were born with doesn't work, doctors can put in an artificial one.

Two Names—Same System

The circulatory system is also called the *cardiovascular system. Cardio* means "related to the heart." *Vascular* means "a system of channels or vessels." So the cardiovascular system is the system with the heart and vessels that carry blood—otherwise known as the circulatory system.

Like other muscles, the heart can be built up and made stronger. You can strengthen your heart muscle by doing aerobic exercise. Aerobic exercise is any activity that makes your heartbeat and breathing increase for at least several minutes. It gives the heart and lungs a workout. Running, swimming, dancing, and cycling are all forms of aerobic exercise.

If you strengthen your heart muscle, you make the heart a stronger, more powerful pump. Then it doesn't need to pump as often to circulate blood around the body. Highly trained athletes who do lots of aerobic exercise have slower heart rates than couch potatoes. Normal heart rates range from 60 to 100 beats a minute for adults. But serious athletes can lower their heart rates to 40 to 45 beats a minute. This means their heart is working half as hard. So to make sure you have the strongest pump possible, give your heart a good workout on a regular basis.

According to the World Health Organization, physical inactivity is a risk factor threatening health throughout the world.

CHAPTER 2

Journey Through the Vessels

A *vessel* is something used for carrying things. Ships are vessels that carry people and goods. A container for carrying liquids is a vessel. In your body, vessels are the tubes that carry your blood to and from the heart and throughout the body. There are three different kinds of vessels—arteries, **capillaries**, and veins. They connect to one another, but each is built differently and has a different job.

The flow of your blood through the vessels is like automobile traffic. The large veins and arteries are like superhighways. They branch into smaller highways and even smaller roads. The capillaries are like neighborhood streets. All blood vessels are one-way streets. They either carry blood to your heart or away from it.

Try This!

To get a good look at your blood vessels, find a mirror. Open your mouth, and curl your tongue up so you can see the underside. Check out the different blood vessels. The pinkish ones are arteries. The blue ones are veins. Capillaries are too small to be seen with your eyes alone.

Arteries

Arteries carry blood away from the heart. Since the blood has just visited the lungs, it is full of oxygen and bright red in color. It is the arteries' job to take this oxygen-rich blood to all parts of the body.

The word *artery* comes from an old Greek word meaning "air pipe." When ancient Greeks looked at the arteries of the dead, they seemed empty. The Greeks thought this meant the pipes were for circulating air around the body.

Blood leaves the heart through a huge artery called the *aorta*. The aorta is shaped like the handle of a cane and is as big around as your thumb. It curves up from the left ventricle and down in front of the backbone.

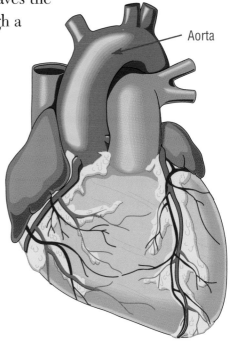

Aorta

The aorta handles the powerful surge of blood coming out of the left ventricle. Blood rushing into the aorta moves with enough force to push it to all parts of your body—even way out to the tips of your fingers and toes. Blood roars through the aorta with pressure strong enough to send water six feet into the air.

Arteries have thick, muscular walls to handle the strong, surging pressure. They can also stretch as the blood pours through.

The aorta branches out into smaller arteries. These arteries divide many times into even smaller arteries as they spread around your body. Some go to the heart muscle to take it food and oxygen. Others go to the rest of the body. The smallest branches are called *arterioles*.

Arteries are the blood vessels you press on to feel your heart rate, or pulse. Arteries swell with every heartbeat and shrink between beats. Veins don't do that.

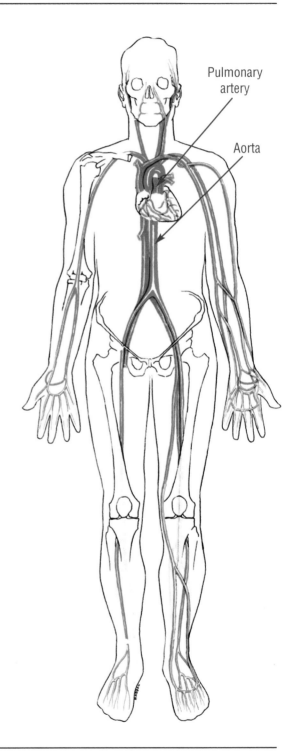

Pulmonary artery

Aorta

Most arteries are far below the skin. They are buried for protection, since arteries spurt out blood when they're cut. The body does have a few places, called *pulse points*, where an artery is close to the surface. If you put your fingers over a pulse point, you can feel the throb of the blood rushing through. Your wrists, insides of your elbows, neck, jaw, temples (sides of your forehead), feet, and backs of your knees all have pulse points.

Try This!

Find one of your pulse points. The neck and wrist are usually the easiest spots. Place your index (pointer) and middle fingers in the area and press lightly. Don't use your thumb. It has a pretty strong pulse itself that might confuse things. Move your fingers around slowly until you feel your pulse.

A pulse rate, or speed, is measured in beats per minute. Once you find your pulse, time yourself to figure out your pulse rate. There are several ways to do this. You can count the beats for a whole minute. Or you can time yourself for half a minute and multiple by two. A quick way is to count the pulse for six seconds and then multiply by ten since there are sixty seconds in a minute. You might want to try all three of these methods (or create others of your own) and compare your results. Is your pulse rate the same no matter which way you count it? (It should be!)

Capillaries

While arteries carry blood away from the heart, they don't actually drop off supplies or pick up wastes from the cells. Only capillaries do that. Arterioles link up to the capillaries. Capillaries are the narrowest blood vessels of all. They are so thin that you can't see them without a microscope and even tiny red blood cells have to move single file through them. Capillary walls are only one cell thick. Oxygen, **nutrients**, carbon dioxide, and other waste materials can easily pass in and out of the capillaries, right through their walls.

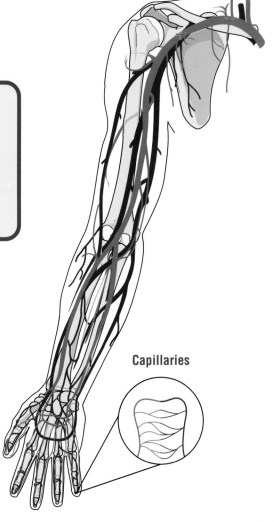

Capillaries

Blushing Capillaries

While you can't see capillaries with your eye, you can see them when somebody blushes. When a person's face turns red, it's because extra blood is rushing to the capillaries in the face.

There are so many capillaries that every cell in your body is no more than a hair's width away from one. Your body has about ten billion of them!

Arteries are shown in red, and veins are shown in blue.

Veins

Capillaries end at the smallest veins called *venules*. These tiny veins link together to make larger and larger veins. The biggest veins return the blood to the heart.

Blood that's in the veins has already dropped off its oxygen in the cells. Does this make the blood in the veins as blue as it appears? No, actually the blood in veins is a dark purplish red. The skin just makes veins look blue.

Blood in the veins doesn't pulse forcefully the way it does in the arteries. It flows more like a gentle river. So vein walls are not as thick, strong, or stretchy as artery walls.

Veins do, however, bulge out when blood fills them. As blood collects in the veins, they puff up. When the blood passes through, the veins flatten out again.

Try This!

Watch your veins bulge. Raise your hand in a loose fist high above your head. Look at the veins on the back of your hand. They should be flat.

Now lower your fist so that it's hanging down by your side. Look at the same veins. Can you see them bulging under your skin?

The force of the heart's pumping action is weaker by the time it reaches the veins. Since most blood traveling back to the heart is climbing upward, it's also fighting against **gravity**. (Think of the blood heading back toward your heart from your toes or up your arms.) Because of this, veins need a little help to keep the blood moving in the right direction. Muscles near the veins squeeze them when you move and help push the blood along. The veins in your arms and legs even have special valves, or flaps, that close off to make sure the blood doesn't slip backward.

Veins Popping Out

Most of the time, you can see some veins under your skin, but they're beneath the surface. But have you ever noticed blue veins popping out on someone's legs? Those are varicose veins. Varicose veins happen when valves in the veins don't work correctly and too much blood collects in one place for too long. The veins then swell up and pop outward, giving the skin surface a rough and bumpy appearance.

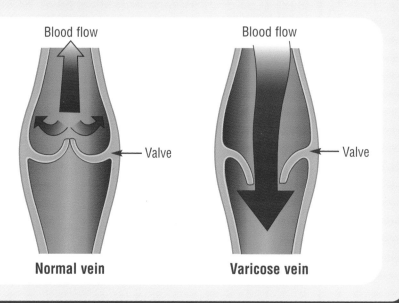

Normal vein

Varicose vein

Heart Highway

Blood that is circulating is similar to a steady flow of traffic. The blood just keeps cruising around your body, from heart to artery to capillary to vein to heart again. When all is working well, there are no accidents and your blood always gets where it's going on time.

Endless Roads

If you could line up all of your arteries, veins, and capillaries from end to end, you could wrap them around the Earth a couple of times and have some left over! A child has about 60,000 miles of blood vessels. An adult has about 100,000 miles of these blood pathways.

Going the Wrong Way?

Remember how the pulmonary artery takes blood to the lungs and the pulmonary vein carries blood away from the lungs? Does this seem backward now that you've learned more about arteries and veins? Shouldn't the pulmonary artery be carrying red blood full of oxygen and the pulmonary vein be carrying "blue" blood with no oxygen?

The pulmonary artery is the only artery that carries oxygen-poor blood. The pulmonary vein is the only vein that carries oxygen-rich blood. So why are they mixed-up? Because all arteries carry blood *away* from the heart, whether it's to the lungs or the body. All veins carry blood *to* the heart from either the body or lungs. It's just like the flow of traffic—you can't go the wrong direction on a one-way street.

Blood Basics

Blood is another word used frequently in our language. "Blood brothers" are close friends who are like family. If you're really mad, then your "blood is boiling." When you're terrified, your "blood runs cold." A "cold-blooded" person has no feelings for others. If you have "blue blood," then you were born into a rich, upper-class family. A "red-blooded" person is someone who is very strong and energetic.

"Blood relations" are family members. Sometimes the word *blood* is used when talking about where our ancestors came from. You might say you have German blood, or Irish blood, or Italian blood.

Like the heart, blood wasn't really understood for a long time, so it came to represent things like the groups we're related to. In reality, the blood from different families and parts of the world is pretty much the same.

Have you ever heard someone say that "blood is thicker than water"? That expression means that family ties are more important than relationships with friends. But the truth is that blood really *is* thicker than water. The four parts of blood—**plasma**, **red blood cells**, **white blood cells**, and **platelets**—make the blood flowing through your body thicker than the water you drink.

Plasma

Blood is made up of plasma and cells. Plasma is the liquid that the cells float in. About 55 percent of your blood is plasma.

Plasma is a pale yellow liquid that is mostly water. Vitamins, nutrients, **hormones**, and other materials that help your body are dissolved in the plasma. As blood circulates, plasma delivers these important substances to the body.

Red Blood Cells

You have billions of red blood cells. One droplet of blood the size of a pinhead holds up to five million red blood cells. Each one is shaped like a round jelly doughnut with a dented center.

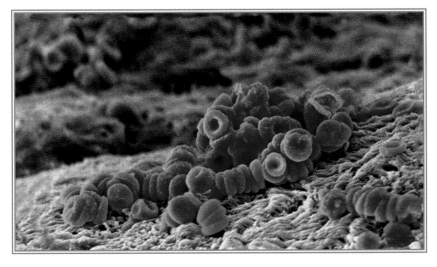

Red blood cells, also known as *erythrocytes*, on an artery wall

Red blood cells only live about four months, but they do a lot of work before they die. Each cell makes about 300,000 trips around your circulatory system before it wears out. When it becomes old or damaged, a cell is broken down and destroyed in your liver and spleen.

Each day, your body makes millions of new red blood cells to replace the old ones. These cells are made in your red bone marrow. Red bone marrow is the soft, jellylike substance in the middle of bones that produces all blood cells.

Red blood cells are flexible. Their centers are very thin. The cells' ability to bend and change shape comes in handy when they have to squeeze through tiny capillaries.

The job of red blood cells is to take oxygen to the cells and pick up carbon dioxide. A substance in the cells called *hemoglobin* latches on to oxygen in the capillaries. When it picks up oxygen, the hemoglobin turns bright red. That's where blood gets its red color. The hemoglobin then carries the oxygen to the cells in the body.

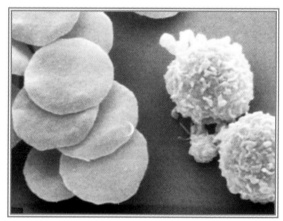

Red blood cells are shown on the left, and white blood cells are on the right.

White Blood Cells

White blood cells aren't really white. They're colorless. These cells are your body's defenders. They fight to protect you from harmful substances.

While there's only one kind of red blood cell, there are many types of white ones. Each type fights for you in a different way. Some release chemicals called *antibodies* that destroy disease-causing substances. Others gobble up **bacteria**. Some stand guard in certain areas of the body, while others patrol the bloodstream until harmful substances invade. Many squeeze out of capillaries and slip between body cells to get to the enemy.

Eventually, all white blood cells die. Some live for only a few hours. Others last for months or even years. You've seen the dead bodies of white blood cells if you've seen pus. When invading bacteria cause an infection, millions of white blood cells rush to the area to fight them. Some of the white blood cells die battling the "bad guys." Pus is a mixture of dead bacteria, the white blood cells that died fighting them, and dead body cells. Pus is found in infected cuts and in the mucus in your nose when you have a cold. Normally mucus is clear, but pus turns it yellow when you're sick.

Platelets

Platelets are actually pieces of cells. Like your other blood cells, platelets are made in your bone marrow. They are created when mother cells pinch off pieces of themselves.

Platelets only last about eight to ten days. Like red blood cells, they're not able to move themselves. They just go with the flow.

You have billions of platelets, but they are very tiny. All of the platelets in your blood at any one time would fill less than two teaspoons.

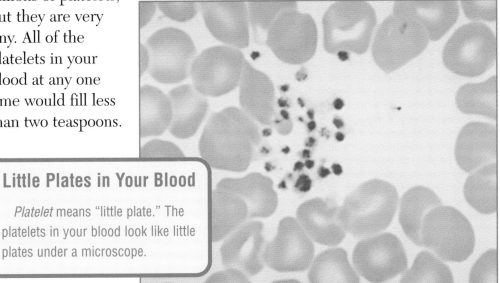

Little Plates in Your Blood

Platelet means "little plate." The platelets in your blood look like little plates under a microscope.

Platelets, also called *thrombocytes*, are surrounded by red blood cells.

Platelets may be small, but they are very important. These cells are responsible for making sure your blood clots, or stops flowing, when necessary. If a blood vessel gets cut, platelets come to your rescue. These sticky cells attach themselves to the edges of a wound. Then they release a chemical into the blood that calls other platelets. All of the platelets clump together to help seal small wounds.

Damaged vessel cells and clumped platelets then release chemicals that trigger the formation of a web of **fibers**. These fibers, called *fibrin*, catch red blood cells, white blood cells, and more platelets. The trapped blood cells form a clot, or hard lump, to stop the bleeding. A scab is a clot on the surface of the skin. A bruise is a clot underneath the skin.

Forming Blood Clots

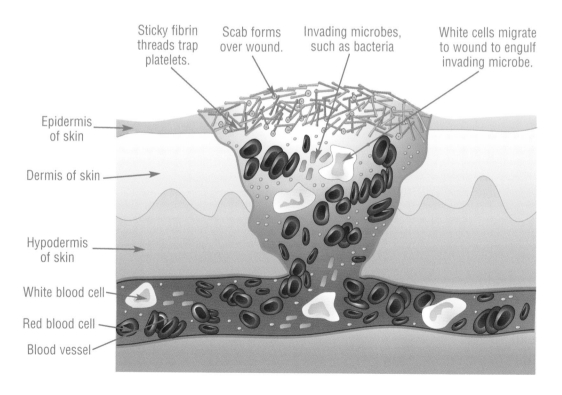

Sticky fibrin threads trap platelets.

Scab forms over wound.

Invading microbes, such as bacteria

White cells migrate to wound to engulf invading microbe.

Epidermis of skin

Dermis of skin

Hypodermis of skin

White blood cell

Red blood cell

Blood vessel

What's Your Type?

Has anyone, perhaps a doctor or a nurse, ever asked you what your blood type is? Did you know the answer? Blood type is determined by the presence or lack of several substances found on the surface of red blood cells. There are eight blood types: A+, A-, B+, B-, AB+, AB-, O+, and O-. (The + stands for positive. The - stands for negative.) If you don't know your blood type, ask your parents or doctor.

How Common Is Your Type?

Once you find out what type of blood you have, check out whether you have a common or uncommon type. This chart shows what percentage of people in the United States have each type of blood.

A+	34 percent
A-	6 percent
B+	9 percent
B-	2 percent
AB+	3 percent
AB-	1 percent
O+	38 percent
O-	7 percent

Take Time to Say Thanks

Most people don't like the sight of blood, especially their own. Blood is often associated with sickness, injury, death, or vampires. But blood is really a miracle fluid. Without it, you wouldn't have life. So the next time a nurse pricks your finger or takes a blood sample, take time to appreciate all blood does for you.

CHAPTER 4

A Busy System

The circulatory system is very busy. It has several important jobs in your body. Its main job is acting as a delivery system for supplies and waste materials. It also delivers chemical messages from one part of your body to another. The circulatory system even helps control your body temperature. Protecting you from harmful substances keeps the system constantly on the move.

A Delivery System

Your body is built out of billions of tiny cells. They come in lots of shapes and sizes. You have skin cells, fat cells, muscle cells, bone cells, and many other types of cells. All of them need a constant supply of energy to stay alive and working. To get this energy, they combine the oxygen from your lungs with the nutrients from your food. But how do the oxygen and food get to the body cells? They hitch a ride in the bloodstream. Your blood picks up oxygen from the lungs and nutrients from the small intestines to carry to all the cells in your body.

Food in Your Blood?

How do nutrients from the food you eat get into your blood? Nutrients enter your bloodstream by passing through the walls of your small intestine into nearby capillaries.

When the cells have finished combining food with oxygen to make energy, they end up with useless waste products. That's no problem for your circulatory system! The system just whisks them away while it's dropping off fresh food and oxygen. It doesn't even slow down or ask for a tip.

Where do these waste materials go? Carbon dioxide is carried back to the lungs. From there, you **exhale** it with each breath. Other wastes are carried to the liver and kidneys, which work together to get rid of harmful substances.

A Message Taker

Blood carries messages from one part of the body to another. Yes, your organs do talk to one another. They send chemical messages in substances called *hormones*. Your pancreas, for example, might send a message to the liver saying there is too much sugar in the blood. The liver gets the message and starts removing sugar from the blood and storing it for later use. Hormones control many of your body functions. They couldn't do this without the help of the circulatory system.

A Body Thermometer

Try jogging in place until you're breathing hard. Look at your face in the mirror. What do you notice?

Run your hand under hot (but not burning) water. What color does your hand turn?

Why do these color changes occur? Because your circulatory system acts as a temperature control, releasing or trapping heat when necessary.

Blood carries heat throughout your body. It cools off parts that are too hot and warms up parts that are too cold. When your body heats up, blood vessels open wider to let more blood flow to the skin. The skin releases the extra heat into the air. If your body cools down, blood vessels in the skin shrink to keep heat from escaping.

When you jogged in place or ran your hand under hot water, blood flow increased to let the extra heat out. When blood rushes to a certain area of the skin, the skin appears red or flushed.

If you're outside in cold temperatures and your body doesn't have enough heat to go around, the circulatory system directs your blood to make sure that the most important parts stay warm. The brain receives the heat it needs, even if that means your nose, fingers, and toes freeze.

A healthy circulatory system protects against hypothermia, a serious condition where body temperature falls well below normal.

A Protector

Last, but not least, the circulatory system acts as your personal bodyguard. White blood cells destroy harmful invaders. Platelets seal up wounds so you don't lose too much blood. This team of defenders keeps your body healthy and safe.

A Healthy Heart and Circulatory System

Sit quietly, and imagine your heart beating in your chest. Place your hand over your heart, and feel the steady pounding. Take your pulse, and think about the blood circulating through your blood vessels at this very moment. Amazing, isn't it? So amazing that it's important to do all you can to make sure your heart, blood vessels, and blood stay strong and healthy.

Blood Pressure

If you've been to a doctor lately, you've probably had your blood pressure checked. The doctor or nurse used a sphygmomanometer. A cuff was placed around your upper arm and inflated until it squeezed your arm tightly. Do you know why this is done?

Blood pressure is the force of blood pushing against the walls of the arteries. To check this force, the cuff squeezes tight enough to stop the flow of blood in a main artery in your arm. Then the doctor or nurse listens with a stethoscope to the artery just below the cuff until he or she can hear the pulse come back when the air is let out. A sphygmomanometer gives two measurements—systolic pressure and diastolic pressure. The systolic pressure measures the highest pressure on the artery walls when the blood pumped through. The diastolic pressure tells how low the pressure was when the heart relaxed between beats.

When your heart has to work harder to pump blood throughout your body, your blood pressure increases. This is called *hypertension* or "having high blood pressure." Several things can cause high blood pressure. Sometimes the arteries become narrower, so blood flow is more difficult. Other times, the body has more blood than normal, so the heart has to work harder to move the excess blood throughout the body. A faster heartbeat can also increase the force of blood against the artery walls.

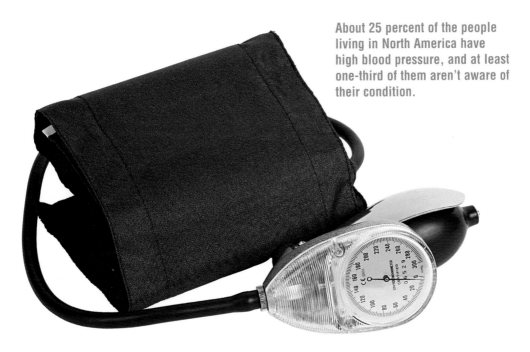

About 25 percent of the people living in North America have high blood pressure, and at least one-third of them aren't aware of their condition.

Temporary high blood pressure can be caused by fear, excitement, stress, or exercise. Often your blood pressure is higher than normal at the doctor's office if you're nervous.

Long-term high blood pressure has several causes. Sometimes it's inherited, or passed down, from your parents or grandparents. Other times, it's the result of kidney disease, heart disease, or other problems. Lifestyle can also contribute to high blood pressure. Eating unhealthy foods, smoking, not exercising, or having a lot of stress in your life can lead to high blood pressure.

No matter what the cause, long-term high blood pressure can be dangerous. It can cause heart attacks, strokes, and other serious illnesses. This type of high blood pressure must be controlled. Cutting down on salt, eating healthy foods, exercising, and taking medication can lower high blood pressure.

The Silent Killer

High blood pressure is sometimes called "the silent killer" because it rarely gives any warning that it's damaging blood vessels until it's too late.

Cardiovascular Diseases

Diseases of the heart and blood vessels are the number one cause of death in the United States. Heart attacks and strokes are the most common of these diseases. Both are caused when blood flow is blocked in the arteries.

A fatty material called *cholesterol* can attach itself to the inside walls of arteries. The liver has the ability to make cholesterol when it's needed. The problem occurs when a person eats foods that contain more cholesterol than the body needs. Red meat, whole milk, cheese, eggs, butter, and many junk foods contain high amounts of cholesterol.

Excess cholesterol that builds up on artery walls is called *plaque*. Plaque makes the arteries narrower. Artery walls also become stiffer and less elastic, or stretchy. This condition is called *arteriosclerosis*, or hardening of the arteries. When the arteries harden, blood can't flow through as easily. Blood clots can form and block these narrow passages.

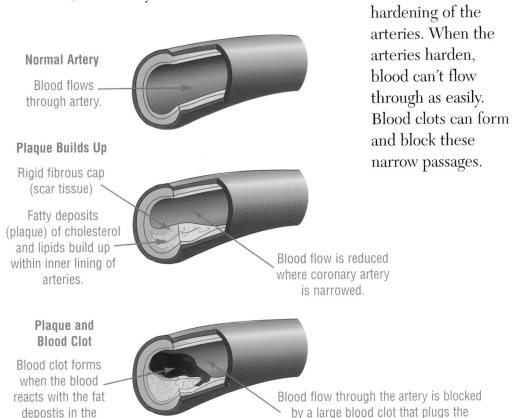

Normal Artery

Blood flows through artery.

Plaque Builds Up

Rigid fibrous cap (scar tissue)

Fatty deposits (plaque) of cholesterol and lipids build up within inner lining of arteries.

Blood flow is reduced where coronary artery is narrowed.

Plaque and Blood Clot

Blood clot forms when the blood reacts with the fat depostis in the artery wall.

Blood flow through the artery is blocked by a large blood clot that plugs the already-narrowed artery.

The arteries that feed the heart are called *coronary arteries*. If one of these arteries is blocked, part of the heart may not receive enough blood. That part of the heart is damaged or can even die. This is called a *heart attack*.

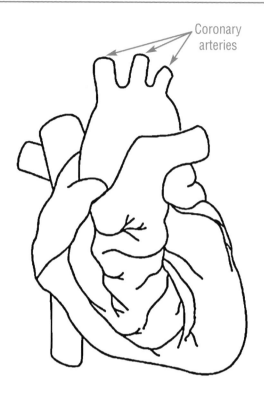

Coronary arteries

The Heart Wears a Crown

Corona means "crown." The coronary arteries leading to the heart look like they form a crown around the top of the heart.

Plaque can block blood vessels in other parts of the body too. A stroke happens when a blood vessel is broken or blocked in the brain. This cuts off the supply of blood to the brain. The part of the brain that was fed by that blood vessel is damaged, causing a stroke. Strokes can be mild or very serious. It depends on what part of the brain is damaged and how much damage is done.

Getting Rid of "Bad" Blood

For hundreds of years, doctors tried to cure sick people by draining blood out of them. This practice was called *bloodletting*. Doctors thought that if they let some of the "bad" blood out, a patient would get better. In reality, it often made patients weaker and sometimes killed them. Finally, in the 1800s, doctors stopped bleeding patients because they realized that it didn't work.

Heart-Healthy Habits

Your age, gender, race, and family history are all factors in cardiovascular diseases that can't be changed. However, several important causes of these diseases *can* be controlled. It's up to you to do what you can to keep your heart and blood vessels healthy.

Eating junk food may taste good, but it isn't good for your circulatory system. Junk food is high in calories, salt, sugar, and fat. All of these things can contribute to heart disease. Eating too much junk food can also lead to being overweight. Extra weight puts a strain on your heart. Instead of eating junk food, try eating dairy products that are lower in fat, lean meats, whole grains, fruits, and vegetables. These foods make your heart happy.

Exercise is another key factor in keeping your heart healthy. Exercise strengthens your heart, lungs, and other muscles. It also helps lower blood pressure and stress. So dance, swim, play basketball, or do whatever exercise you enjoy. It will do your heart good.

If you're a person who gets easily upset over every little thing, your risk of having high blood pressure, a heart attack, or a stroke may increase. Finding healthy ways to deal with stress, such as exercise or talking to a friend, can help lower this risk.

Smoking cigarettes greatly increases your chances of having a stroke or heart attack someday. Smoking increases your blood pressure. The nicotine in cigarettes causes small blood vessels to narrow. Your heart has to work harder to pump your blood when you smoke. So give your heart a break and don't smoke.

Conclusion
Circulate the News!

The circulatory system is remarkable. Blood is pumped around the body by a mighty muscle known as the heart. Blood surges from the heart through the arteries. Arteries divide over and over as they spread throughout your body. They link to tiny capillaries. Capillaries' thin walls let the oxygen, hormones, and nutrients seep into surrounding cells. Carbon dioxide and other waste products from those cells pass through capillary walls into the blood. The blood whisks them away in veins to be removed from the body by your liver, kidneys, and lungs. Whew! It's tiring just thinking of everything your circulatory system does for you.

Blood is a pretty amazing material too. It circulates oxygen and nutrients while keeping an eye on your body temperature. The parts of the blood have special jobs to keep you healthy. Red blood cells and plasma handle the blood's delivery system. White blood cells protect and defend you from germ invaders 24 hours a day. Platelets rush to injuries to stop blood loss.

Taking care of your circulatory system by eating healthy foods, exercising, reducing stress, and not smoking is very important. So spread the news about protecting your circulatory system. You'll be glad you did, because your real heart is far more valuable than a heart of gold could ever be.

Internet Connections and Related Reading for the Circulatory System

http://kidshealth.org/kid/body/heart_SW.html

Explore the circulatory system at this site just for kids. Includes lots of diagrams and fun facts.

http://www.innerbody.com/image/cardov.html

Click on the parts of the circulatory system for a description of each one.

http://vilenski.org/science/humanbody/hb_html/circ_system.html

Go on a "Human Body Adventure." Check out the information about the circulatory system, heart, veins, and arteries. Then take a quiz to see how much you've learned.

http://science.howstuffworks.com/heart.htm

Learn how the heart works by touring this site that has lots of information, diagrams, and interesting facts.

http://science.howstuffworks.com/blood.htm

Get your blood basics here, including blood circulation, blood cells, and blood types.

Blood by Steve Parker. Offers students a comprehensive picture of how blood works in the body. Millbrook Press, 1997. [RL 5 IL 4–6] (3110806 HB)

Hear Your Heart by Paul Showers. All the facts about your heart. Day and night it keeps on working, pumping blood through your body. HarperCollins, 2001. [RL 3 IL K–5] (8746701 PB 8746702 CC)

Human Body by Steve Parker. An Eyewitness Book on the human body. Dorling Kindersley, 1993. [RL 7.7 IL 3–8] (5868906 HB)

•RL = Reading Level
•IL = Interest Level
Perfection Learning's catalog numbers are included for your ordering convenience. PB indicates paperback. CC indicates Cover Craft. HB indicates hardback.

Glossary

artery (AR ter ee) blood vessel that carries blood away from the heart

atrium (AY tree uhm) upper chamber of the heart

bacteria (bak TEAR ee uh) tiny organisms (living things) that can cause illness and disease

blood (bluhd) liquid that delivers oxygen and other substances to the body and picks up waste materials

blood vessel (bluhd VES uhl) tube that carries blood to or from the heart

capillary (KAP uh lair ee) blood vessel that delivers oxygen and nutrients to the cells and picks up waste materials (see separate entry for *cell*)

cell (sel) smallest unit of living matter

exhale (EKS hayl) to breathe out

fiber (FEYE ber) long, thin, threadlike structure

gravity (GRAV uh tee) force that pulls objects toward the center of the Earth

heart (hart) muscle that pumps blood to the body

hormone (HOR mohn) substance that sends messages to the cells (see separate entry for *cell*)

nutrient (NOO tree ent) material that living things need to live and grow

pacemaker (PAYS may ker) object that controls the rhythm or speed of something

plasma (PLAZ mah) liquid in blood that carries cells and other dissolved substances (see separate entry for *cell*)

platelet (PLAYT let) cell that helps blood clot, or stop flowing (see separate entry for *cell*)

red blood cell (red bluhd sel) cell that carries oxygen from the lungs to the cells in the body (see separate entry for *cell*)

vein (vayn) blood vessel that carries blood back to the heart (see separate entry for *blood vessel*)

ventricle (VEN trik uhl) lower chamber of the heart

white blood cell (wheyet bluhd sel) cell that attacks harmful substances in the body (see separate entry for *cell*)

Index